Fact Finders®

The
Solar System
and Beyond

The Dwarf Planets

by Steve Kortenkamp

Consultant:
Dr. Ilia I. Roussev
Associate Astronomer
Institute for Astronomy
University of Hawaii at Manoa

CAPSTONE PRESS
a capstone imprint

Fact Finders are published by Capstone Press,
151 Good Counsel Drive, P.O. Box 669, Mankato, Minnesota 56002.
www.capstonepub.com

Library of Congress Cataloging-in-Publication Data
Kortenkamp, Steve.
 The dwarf planets / by Steve Kortenkamp.
 p. cm.—(Fact finders. The solar system and beyond)
 Includes bibliographical references and index.
 Summary: "Describes the five dwarf planets in our solar system, including the birth of the solar system
and the dwarf planets' orbits around the Sun"—Provided by publisher.
 ISBN 978-1-4296-5397-8 (library binding)
 ISBN 978-1-4296-6242-0 (paperback)
 1. Dwarf planets—Juvenile literature. I. Title. II. Series.
 QB698.K67 2011
 523.49—dc22
                                                              2010026023

Editorial Credits

Jennifer Besel, editor; Heidi Thompson, designer; Laura Manthe, production specialist

Photo Credits

Alamy: Friedrich Saurer, 3, 19 (inset), Mary Evans Picture Library, 5, Peter Arnold, Inc., 29; Comstock
Images, 7 (moon, planet); Dreamstime/Pseudolongino, cover, 1; ESA/B. Dintinjana and J. Skvarc,
7 (comet); NASA, 22; NASA, Ben Zellner (Georgia Southern University), Peter Thomas (Cornell
University), 7 (asteroid); NASA, CalTech, 25; NASA, ESA, H. Weaver (JHU/APL), A. Stern (SwRI),
The HST Pluto Companion Search Team, 19; NASA, ESA, J. Parker (Southwest Research Institute),
17 (inset); NASA, ESA, M. Brown (California Institute of Technology), 25 (inset); NASA, JHUAPL,
SwRI, 27; NASA, JPL-Caltech, R.Hurt (SSC-Caltech), 23; NASA/JPL-Caltech/R. Hurt (SSC), 11, T. Pyle
(SSC), 8–9; Photo Researchers, Inc: Chris Butler, 15, 17, Detlev van Ravenswaay, 7 (dwarf planet), John
R. Foster, 20–21

Artistic Effects

iStockphoto: appleuzr, Dar Yang Yan, Nickilford

Printed in the United States of America in North Mankato, Minnesota.
062011   006222R

Table of Contents

Chapter 1

Is It a Planet?

More than 200 years ago, astronomers were just beginning to understand our solar system. They studied the distances between the planets they could see. Based on the distances, astronomers believed there was a planet between Mars and Jupiter. They searched for the hidden planet for years. Finally, one of them saw a tiny planet that became known as Ceres.

But there was a problem. Astronomers had expected Ceres to be alone in its orbit. Ceres was definitely not alone. Three more little planets were found near it. Then over the years, astronomers discovered more and more small objects nearby. After 50 years, they changed their minds. Astronomers decided that Ceres and all the objects near it were asteroids, not planets.

orbit: the path an object follows as it goes around the Sun

asteroid: a large space rock that moves around the Sun

FACT: Ceres was discovered in 1801 by an astronomer in Sicily, an island near Italy.

Fast-forward to 2006. Astronomers had the same problem with Pluto. For 75 years everyone called Pluto the ninth planet. But with better technology, thousands of objects were found near Pluto. One of these objects is bigger than Pluto itself. Discovery of these new objects made astronomers change their minds again. They decided that Pluto was not a planet. Instead, they called Pluto, Ceres, and three other objects dwarf planets.

Defining a Dwarf Planet

In 2006 astronomers created rules to define what space objects should be called. They also created a new category called dwarf planets. But what makes dwarf planets different from planets, moons, or asteroids?

First, planets must orbit around the Sun. They can't orbit around anything else. Moons are not planets for this very reason. For example, Earth's moon orbits our planet, not the Sun.

Second, planets must be round. Almost all asteroids have uneven, crooked shapes. They look like giant potatoes. Asteroids are not planets.

Finally, planets cannot have other big objects nearby that also orbit the Sun. Ceres and Pluto aren't planets because they have big neighbors.

Scientists know of five objects in the solar system that follow the first two rules. But they have large neighbors. Astronomers call objects like these dwarf planets.

asteroid

comet

	Orbit the Sun	Have a round shape	Have no large objects near their orbits
Asteroids and Comets	X		
Dwarf Planets	X	X	
Moons		X	
Planets	X	X	X

dwarf planet

planet

moon

Chapter 2

In the Solar System

About 5 billion years ago, our Sun did not exist. There was no solar system. Instead, there was a **molecular cloud**. Part of this cloud slowly began to cave in. Most of the gas and dust in the shrinking cloud collected in the center and got very hot. When the gas in the center reached 18 million degrees Fahrenheit (10 million degrees Celsius) it started to burn. Our Sun was born!

molecular cloud: a giant cloud made mostly of hydrogen atoms bound together

Some of the gas and dust in the shrinking cloud fell into a flat disk. The disk swirled around the new star. In the disk, dust stuck together and grew into rocks. Then rocks clumped together forming boulders. Soon some of the growing boulders were pulled into a round shape, becoming dwarf planets.

The dwarf planets bumped into other boulders. They soon grew into a few small rocky planets. This bumping formed the inner planets of the solar system—Mercury, Venus, Earth, and Mars. Ceres and the asteroids are leftover rocks from the inner part of the disk.

Farther out from the Sun, the disk was bigger and held more dust. The disk was also a lot colder. Some of the gas froze into ice that mixed with the dust. Bigger planets formed from this icy material. The bigger planets had strong **gravity**. They pulled in hydrogen and helium gases from the disk. These outer planets grew into Jupiter, Saturn, Uranus, and Neptune. Pluto and the other small objects near it never grew into giant planets.

Dwarf planets, asteroids, and comets are leftover from the time when the planets formed. Once in a while, pieces of these leftover rocks fall to Earth as meteorites.

gravity: a force that pulls objects together

FACT: Chemicals in meteorites are like pictures of the past. By studying the chemicals, scientists know that our solar system finished forming about 4.5 billion years ago.

Spinning Around

The Sun's gravity keeps everything in the solar system orbiting around it. The farther a planet or dwarf planet is from the Sun, the longer it takes to go around it. Earth orbits the Sun in about 365 days. We call that time a year. Ceres is about 2½ times farther away from the Sun than Earth. It takes 1,680 days for Ceres to go around the Sun once. The dwarf planet Eris needs more than 550 Earth years to complete its orbit.

Everything orbiting around the Sun has daytime and nighttime. That's because planets, dwarf planets, asteroids, and comets are all **rotating** like spinning tops. Earth takes 24 hours to rotate one time. We call that a day. Ceres spins faster than Earth. A day on Ceres lasts only nine hours. A day on Pluto lasts for more than 150 hours.

rotate: to turn around and around

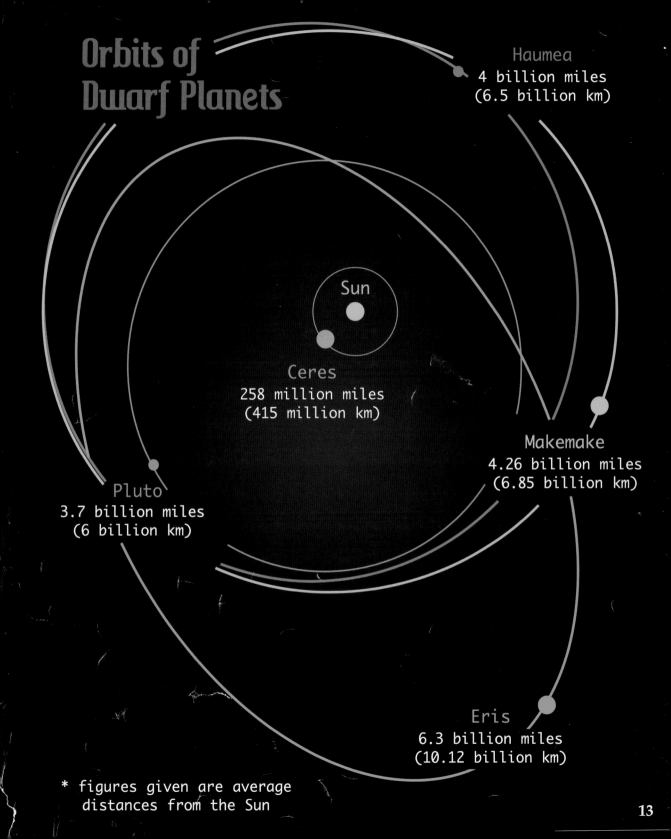

Orbits of Dwarf Planets

Haumea
4 billion miles
(6.5 billion km)

Sun

Ceres
258 million miles
(415 million km)

Makemake
4.26 billion miles
(6.85 billion km)

Pluto
3.7 billion miles
(6 billion km)

Eris
6.3 billion miles
(10.12 billion km)

* figures given are average
distances from the Sun

Chapter 3

The Dwarf Planets

As of 2009, scientists have identified five dwarf planets in our solar system. But they really don't know much about them. Dwarf planets are so far away, even the strongest telescopes can't see much of them.

Ceres

Ceres orbits around the Sun in the solar system's asteroid belt. There are millions of rocky asteroids in this area. But pictures of Ceres taken with the Hubble Space Telescope prove that Ceres is round. That round shape makes Ceres a dwarf planet.

Only about 590 miles (950 kilometers) across, Ceres is the smallest dwarf planet. Compare that to our planet. Earth is about 8,000 miles (12,875 km) across.

FACT: Ceres is the largest object in the asteroid belt.

Compared to Earth, Ceres is tiny.

Pictures of Ceres show it is grayish-brown in color with fuzzy light and dark patches. Its surface may look a lot like our Moon. Scientists think Ceres may be covered in **craters** that form when asteroids crash into it.

crater: a hole made when large pieces of rock crash into the surface of a space object

Ceres orbits about 250 million miles (400 million km) away from the Sun. At that distance the Sun can only warm Ceres to about -36°F (-38°C). That means Ceres might have a lot of ice. Astronomers believe the dwarf planet has a rocky core. Around the core may be a thick layer of ice. Some astronomers believe there could also be a layer with liquid water. If so, then Ceres could have an ocean under its frozen, dusty surface. Ceres may also have a very thin atmosphere of water vapor surrounding it. At night on Ceres, the water in the atmosphere would turn to frost and fall on the surface.

core: the inner part of a dwarf planet

atmosphere: the gases that surround a dwarf planet

an artist's illustration of what Ceres might look like

FACT: Since it was discovered, Ceres has been called a comet, a planet, an asteroid, and a dwarf planet.

image of Ceres taken by the Hubble Space Telescope

Pluto

Past Neptune is an area called the trans-Neptunian region. This region is about 3 billion miles (5 billion km) away. From that far away, our Sun just looks like a very bright star. There are billions of icy objects in this region. Pluto was the first one ever seen. Pictures from the Hubble Space Telescope show that Pluto is round. The dwarf planet also has light and dark patches on its surface.

Pluto is about 1,400 miles (2,300 km) across. Orbiting around this dwarf planet are three moons. Pluto's biggest moon is Charon. It is more than half the size of Pluto. No other moon is this big when compared to the planet it orbits. Two smaller moons named Nix and Hydra also orbit Pluto.

FACT: Pluto and Charon actually orbit each other. Charon doesn't orbit Pluto like the other moons. Some scientists believe that once they have more information, Charon will be called a dwarf planet too.

an artist's illustration of what
Pluto might look like

Pluto

Nix

Charon

Hydra

image of Pluto and its moons taken
by the Hubble Space Telescope

Scientists study the way Pluto's moons orbit the dwarf planet. The moons' movements help astronomers learn about Pluto's gravity. Astronomers can figure out what Pluto is made of by its gravity's strength. Pluto is about half rock and half ice. The rock is mostly in Pluto's core. A thick layer of ice surrounds the core. Just like Ceres, there may be an ocean of water under the frozen surface of Pluto. Astronomers wonder if anything is living in that ocean.

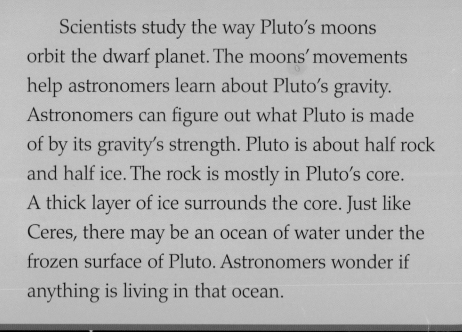

Charon

surface of Pluto

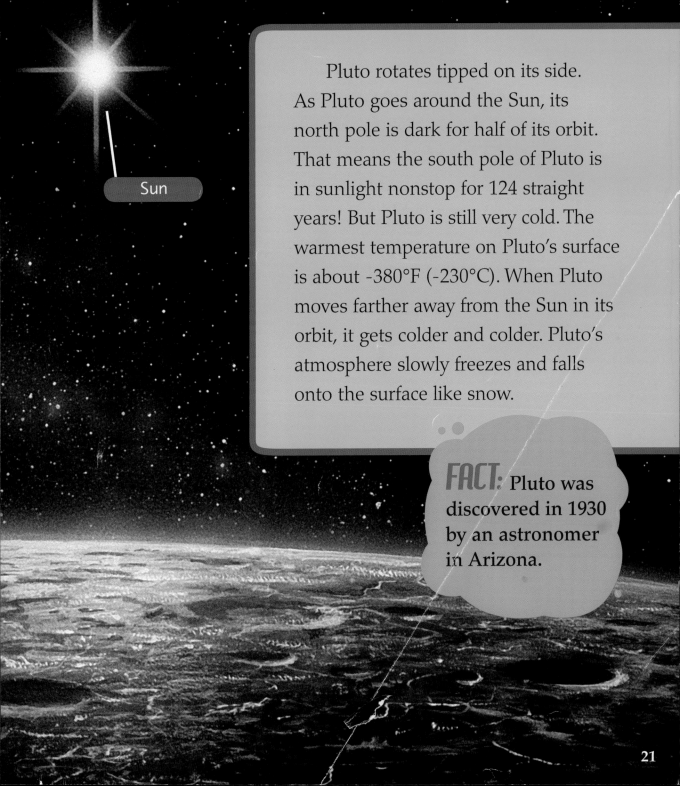

Sun

Pluto rotates tipped on its side. As Pluto goes around the Sun, its north pole is dark for half of its orbit. That means the south pole of Pluto is in sunlight nonstop for 124 straight years! But Pluto is still very cold. The warmest temperature on Pluto's surface is about -380°F (-230°C). When Pluto moves farther away from the Sun in its orbit, it gets colder and colder. Pluto's atmosphere slowly freezes and falls onto the surface like snow.

FACT: Pluto was discovered in 1930 by an astronomer in Arizona.

Haumea

The dwarf planet Haumea (how-MAY-ah) is a strange object. Pictures show that Haumea is shaped like a football. It is shaped this way because it is spinning very fast. A day on Haumea only lasts four hours! This fast rotation stretches out the dwarf planet's shape. If Haumea were not spinning so fast it would be round, so astronomers still call it a dwarf planet.

Two tiny moons orbit Haumea. Just like with Pluto, astronomers can tell what Haumea is made of by how these moons move. Haumea has a thin layer of ice on its surface. But on the inside, it is almost all rock.

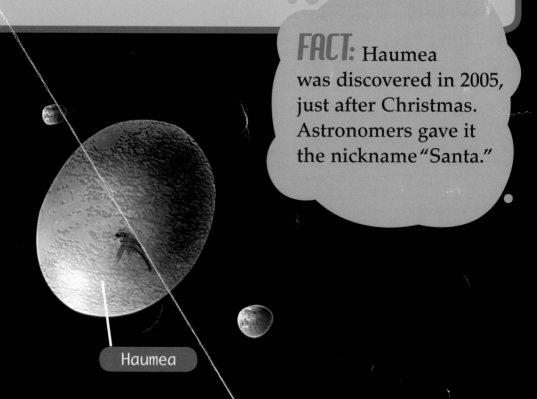

FACT: Haumea was discovered in 2005, just after Christmas. Astronomers gave it the nickname "Santa."

Haumea

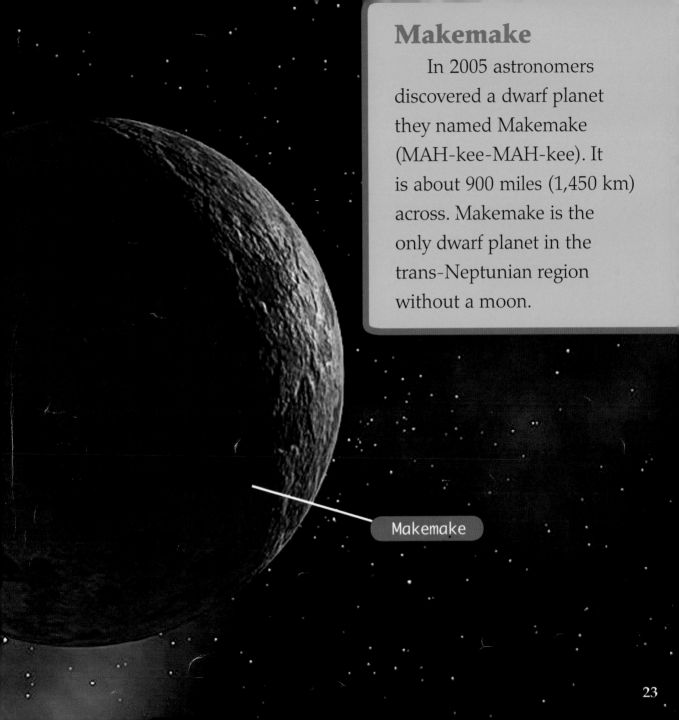

Makemake

In 2005 astronomers discovered a dwarf planet they named Makemake (MAH-kee-MAH-kee). It is about 900 miles (1,450 km) across. Makemake is the only dwarf planet in the trans-Neptunian region without a moon.

Makemake

Eris

Eris is the largest dwarf planet in the solar system. It is about 1,500 miles (2,400 km) across. Eris is about 6 billion miles (10 billion km) away from the Sun. At this distance the dwarf planet is extremely cold at about -400°F (-240°C). Its atmosphere has completely frozen and fallen onto the surface as snow.

Pictures of Eris show a little moon orbiting the dwarf planet. The moon is named Dysnomia, and it orbits Eris in about 16 days. From the way Dysnomia moves, astronomers can tell what Eris is made of. The dwarf planet is about half rock and half ice, just like Pluto.

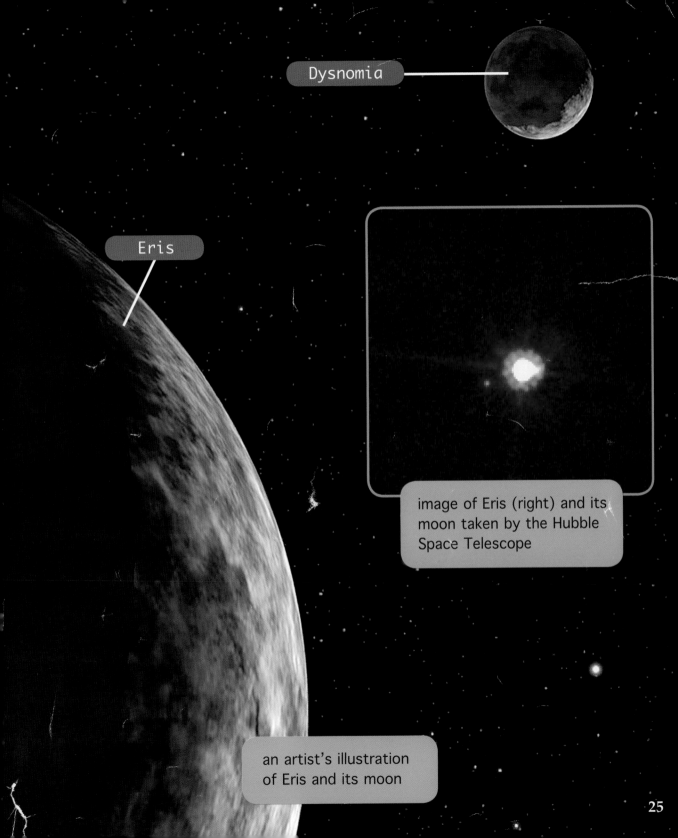

Dysnomia

Eris

image of Eris (right) and its moon taken by the Hubble Space Telescope

an artist's illustration of Eris and its moon

25

Chapter 4

Studying Dwarf Planets

Scientists use space **probes** to explore our solar system. Many probes have been sent to all eight planets. Now two new probes are on their way to study Ceres and Pluto.

The space probe *Dawn* was launched in 2007. In 2011 it will go into orbit around an asteroid named Vesta. Vesta is one of the "planets" discovered with Ceres more than 200 years ago. Astronomers want to study Vesta to learn more about where the asteroids came from. *Dawn* will then move on to Ceres in 2015. When it arrives, astronomers will have their first close-up look at the dwarf planet.

probe: a small vehicle used to explore in space

illustration of *New Horizons* at Pluto

In 2015 the probe *New Horizons* will fly by Pluto. It will study Pluto's atmosphere and send pictures of Pluto back to Earth. Then *New Horizons* will study other trans-Neptunian objects.

Exciting Science

Astronomers are always discovering new things. Sometimes new discoveries make them change their minds, like with Ceres and Pluto. Astronomers have only named five dwarf planets in the solar system so far. But there are thousands of trans-Neptunian objects that haven't been studied. How many of them are round? Maybe there are hundreds—or even thousands—of dwarf planets that scientists don't know about yet. Maybe someday new discoveries will once again make scientists change what it means to be a planet in our solar system.

Comparing Dwarf Planets

	Length of Day (sunrise to sunrise)	Length of Year (once around the Sun)	Number of moons
Ceres	9 hours	4.6 Earth years	0
Pluto	154 hours	248 Earth years	3
Haumea	4 hours	283 Earth years	2
Makemake	unknown	310 Earth years	0
Eris	unknown	557 Earth years	1

Glossary

asteroid (AS-tuh-royd)—a large space rock that moves around the Sun; most asteroids are not round enough to be called planets

atmosphere (AT-muh-sfeer)—the layer of gases that surrounds some dwarf planets, moons, planets, and stars

core (KOR)—the inner part of a dwarf planet, planet, or star

crater (KRAY-tuhr)—a hole made when large pieces of rock crash into the surface of a dwarf planet, moon, or planet

gravity (GRAV-uh-tee)—a force that pulls objects together; gravity increases as the mass of objects increases or as objects get closer

molecular cloud (muh-LEK-yuh-lur KLOUD)—a cloud trillions of miles across made mostly of hydrogen atoms bound together; new stars form deep within the cores of molecular clouds

orbit (OR-bit)—the path an object follows as it goes around a dwarf planet, planet, or star

probe (PROHB)—a small vehicle used to explore objects in outer space

rotate (ROH-tate)—to turn around and around

Read More

Birch, Robin. *Dwarf Planets*. The New Solar System. New York: Chelsea House Publishers, 2008.

Carson, Mary Kay. *Far-Out Guide to the Icy Dwarf Planets*. Far-Out Guide to the Solar System. Berkeley Heights, N.J.: Enslow Elementary, 2011.

Jefferis, David. *Ice Dwarfs: Pluto and Beyond*. Exploring Our Solar System. New York.: Crabtree Pub., 2009.

Kortenkamp, Steve. *The Planets of Our Solar System*. The Solar System and Beyond. Mankato, Minn.: Capstone Press, 2011.

Internet Sites

FactHound offers a safe, fun way to find Internet sites related to this book. All of the sites on FactHound have been researched by our staff.

Here's all you do:

Visit *www.facthound.com*

Type in this code: 9781429653978

Check out projects, games and lots more at
www.capstonekids.com

Index